Fraud Schemes

Steven M. Bragg

AccountingTools®

ISBN 978-1-64221-212-9

For more information about AccountingTools® products, visit our Web site at www.accountingtools.com.

Table of Contents

About the Author

Steven Bragg, CPA, has been the chief financial officer or controller of four companies, as well as a consulting manager at Ernst & Young. He received a master's degree in finance from Bentley College, an MBA from Babson College, and a Bachelor's degree in Economics from the University of Maine. He has been a two-time president of the Colorado Mountain Club, and is an avid alpine skier, mountain biker, and certified master diver. Mr. Bragg resides in Centennial, Colorado. He has written more than 300 books and courses, including *New Controller Guidebook*, *GAAP Guidebook*, and *Payroll Management*.

Steven maintains the accountingtools.com web site, which contains continuing professional education courses, the Accounting Best Practices podcast, and thousands of articles on accounting subjects.

Chapter 1
Fraud Schemes by Employees

Introduction

This manual is intended to make the business person aware of the broad range of fraud schemes that may be perpetrated against an organization by its employees and outsiders. In this chapter, we focus on frauds that are perpetrated by employees. Since financial statement fraud is quite a large topic, we break that out into the following chapter, and then finish in Chapter 3 with fraud schemes perpetrated by people operating outside of the organization.

In this chapter, we begin with a discussion of the nature of fraud and then work our way through a large number of fraud schemes. The discussion is organized into the following general headings:

- Cash schemes
- Receivable schemes
- Inventory schemes
- Procurement schemes
- Payable schemes
- Human resources schemes
- Executive-level schemes

What is Fraud?

Fraud is a false representation of the facts, resulting in the object of the fraud receiving an injury by acting upon the misrepresented facts. Stated somewhat differently, fraud is trickery used to gain a dishonest advantage over another person. The following synonyms can be used to gain a better understanding of the broad extent of fraud.

Fraud Synonyms

Blackmail	Double-cross	Ploy
Cheat	Extortion	Ruse
Con	Hoax	Scam
Confidence trick	Hoodwink	Sham
Deceit	Misrepresentation	Swindle

Fraud is proven in court by showing that the actions of an individual involved the following elements:

- A false statement of a material fact;
- Knowledge that the statement was untrue;
- Intent by the individual to deceive the victim;
- Reliance by the victim on the statement; and
- Injury sustained by the victim as a result of the preceding actions.

The key element in the preceding definition is *intent*. A company could make false representations in its financial statements simply because the accounting staff made a mistake in compiling certain financial information. This is not fraud (though it may be incompetence), since there was no intent to misstate the financial statements. Conversely, if a controller intentionally reduces the bad debt reserve in order to increase profits and thereby triggers a bonus for the management team, this *is* fraud, because a false statement was intentionally made.

Within a company, an employee can use fraud to steal assets, where facts are misrepresented in order to hide the theft. For example:

- A warehouse employee steals inventory and covers up the theft by recording the inventory in the warehouse tracking system as having been scrapped. The fraudulent action is recording a false transaction.
- A salesperson sells inventory to a customer, takes the cash payment from the customer, and never records the sale. In this case, the fraudulent action is *not* recording the transaction.

Cash Schemes

Cash cannot be uniquely identified and is easily disposed of, so it tends to garner a significant amount of attention from those engaged in fraudulent transactions. The amounts stolen tend to be relatively low, since organizations typically keep only modest amounts on hand to meet their immediate needs. Also, since businesses tend to maintain tight control over their cash, there are fewer opportunities to make away with large sums. Nonetheless, the illicit pursuit of cash is relatively common. In the following sub-sections, we note several fraud schemes that can be used to extract cash from a business.

Skimming (No Recordation)

One of the easier frauds for an employee to perpetrate is to remove a portion of any incoming cash before it can be recorded in a company's books. For example, a salesperson could sell inventory and pocket the proceeds without recording the sale. Skimming is especially common when employees can engage in sales activities from an off-site location, after normal business hours, or where there is little or no management supervision. This approach is most common in retail environments where most sales are in cash.

Skimming is a particular problem when the founders of a business engage in it. By doing so, they are pocketing money for which income taxes will never be paid, while the business reports lower profits. Since these individuals are the founders, they can easily circumvent all controls that might otherwise be in place. A further concern in this case is that founders set the ethical tone for the business, so if employees see them stealing cash, the employees are more likely to do so, too.

The existence of skimming can be detected by tracking the gross margin percentage over time. If inventory is being sold and the proceeds pocketed by employees, then the gross margin percentage should trend lower over time. Fixing the skimming problem can be quite difficult, since a higher level of employee monitoring is required, for which there is a cost that offsets any decline in skimming activity.

One way to minimize skimming is to require payments using credit or debit cards, so that cash is removed from the payment process.

Discounted Sales (Partial Recordation)

A failing of the skimming approach just noted is that inventory leaves the premises without a corresponding sale transaction, resulting in a detectable decline in the gross margin percentage. An employee can instead record a sale in the accounting system in order to log the inventory outflow, but also records a discount against the sale and steals the amount of the discount. For example, an employee sells a widget for $100 and collects $100 from the customer. The person then records the sale as $100, minus a promotional discount of $20, for a net sale of $80. The employee then takes $20. In this case, the only evidence of theft is the presence of an unusually large number of discounts being taken. If the employee engaged in this fraud is careful and only records a few of these discount transactions, the theft will likely not be detected.

The problem can be combatted by requiring management approval for all but the smallest discounts.

Modification of Receipts (Altered Recordation)

If an employee is responsible for all aspects of the cash receipts process, it is not especially difficult for the person to extract incoming cash and then alter the receipts documentation to cover up or obscure the amount of the theft. For example, a few receipts could be selectively damaged, making it impossible for anyone else to reconcile the receipts to the amount actually deposited. If these thefts are kept at a low level, any differences between recorded amounts and actual cash balances will probably be charged to expense with no further investigation.

The main preventive technique to avoid the modification of receipts is to strictly separate responsibility for the various steps in the cash receiving, recordation, and depositing process. By doing so, the person recording receipts has no incentive to alter or destroy records, while the person handling cash has no control over the recordation process. Since there are not enough people in a smaller organization to properly engage in this segregation of duties, smaller enterprises tend to suffer the most from the modification of receipts fraud.

Fake Refunds (Subsequent Recordation)

Cash can be stolen after a sale transaction has been initially recorded. An employee could create a fake refund transaction for a customer and then pocket the payment. For example, an accounting clerk in the receivables area could create a credit memo for a customer, triggering a payment back to the customer. The clerk then extracts the payment from the outgoing pile of checks, forges a signature on the check, signs it over to himself, and deposits the check in his bank account. There are several variations on this concept, such as:

- A product is recorded in the accounting system as having been returned by a customer, which triggers a refund payment.
- A refund is artificially authorized to a customer for a volume discount, which triggers a refund payment.

Fake refunds will only work if there is a control weakness in the system, where the person initiating the refund can reliably intercept the outbound check payment. Otherwise, some of these payments will leak through to the intended customers, who may inquire as to why the payments were sent.

Fake refunds can be stymied if all refund requests must be approved in advance by management and must be accompanied by supporting documentation. In addition, if the fraud involves recording returned goods in the system, ongoing inventory counts should eventually note that the number of inventory units listed in the accounting records as being on hand is routinely higher than the amount actually counted.

Receivable Schemes

Employees can perpetrate several fraud schemes involving accounts receivable. In all cases, the end result is the extraction of cash from the business. Since these situations all involve masking the loss of cash, they can be considered extensions of the cash schemes noted in the preceding section. In the following sub-sections, we note several fraud schemes that involve receivables.

Diversion of Collections on Old Receivables

When customers do not pay invoices for a long period of time, the seller will likely write them off, so there is no longer a receivable balance for these invoices on the books. If a payment eventually arrives that pays for one of these vastly overdue invoices, an employee could steal the check payment and divert the deposit into his own bank account. Since the company already wrote off the invoice, there is no way for the diverted payment to be detected. An enterprising employee can accelerate this process by encouraging the company controller to write off unpaid invoices sooner, giving the employee even more opportunities to harvest incoming payments from customers.

The best way to prevent the diversion of incoming checks is to segregate duties, so that all incoming checks are recorded in the mailroom, which keeps other employees from extracting checks at a later point in the cash receipts process while avoiding detection.

Lapping

Lapping occurs when an employee steals cash by diverting a payment from one customer and then hides the theft by diverting cash from another customer to offset the receivable from the first customer. This type of fraud can be conducted in perpetuity, since newer payments are continually being used to pay for older debts, so that no receivable involved in the fraud ever appears to be that old.

Lapping is most easily engaged in when just one employee is involved in all cash handling and recordation tasks. This situation most commonly arises in a smaller business, where a bookkeeper may be responsible for all accounting tasks.

If these tasks are split among several people, then lapping can only be conducted when two or more employees are involved. Lapping typically requires that the person engaged in the fraud be involved every day, and so does not take any vacation time. Thus, having a person refuse to take the vacation time that they have earned can be considered a possible indicator of the existence of lapping.

Lapping can be detected by conducted a periodic review of the cash receipts records, to trace payments to outstanding receivables. If there is ongoing evidence that cash receipts are routinely being applied against the wrong customer accounts, then either the cashier is astonishingly incompetent or there is an active lapping scheme in progress.

Inventory Schemes

Some inventory schemes differ from the preceding cash and receivable frauds, in that inventory is stolen and must then be sold off to a third party in order to convert it into cash. In some cases where employees have a personal use for the inventory, they may simply steal and retain the goods. One instance in which a perpetrator can directly extract cash from an inventory fraud is when proceeds from the sale of scrap are diverted. Several inventory schemes are described in the following sub-sections.

Incorrect Receipt Fraud

An employee at the receiving dock can collude with a delivery person to sign for incoming materials at a quantity that is greater than the amount actually received. The delivery person retains the difference, sells off the inventory, and splits the proceeds with the receiving person.

This arrangement can be detected by reviewing situations in which inventory records indicate a higher balance than is actually present, and then tracing back to the receiving records to determine which employee signed for the goods. However, this detective work can be defeated if the receiving clerk forges the signatures of other receiving staff on the receiving documents.

Product Replacement Fraud

Employees can steal significant amounts of inventory if they create fake credit memos to customers that have allegedly returned defective goods. The supposedly returned items are designated in the warehouse records as having been scrapped, and are then stolen from the warehouse. The employees liquidate the stolen inventory and pocket the proceeds. This fraud will only work when there is collusion between the warehouse staff (which steals the inventory) and selected accounting staff (who process the credit memos).

This fraud will create a spike in the inventory returns level, and should trigger an investigation by the product design team, which will want to know why so many products are being returned. Given these risks, the perpetrators will have the best chance of success if they keep the theft level fairly low, so that the extra credit memos only register as a slight uptick in the historical product returns rate.

Diversion of Scrap Payments

Manufacturing firms typically throw their metal scrap into a bin. A scrap dealer periodically removes this scrap, paying for the weight of metal removed. Since the scrap dealer pays on the spot, it is not difficult for an employee to intercept this payment at the warehouse dock area. The amount of receipts from scrap dealers is usually quite a small amount in proportion to the total cost of goods sold, so many companies do not bother with controls in this area, allowing for unmitigated theft.

There are several ways to address the diversion of scrap payments. One approach is to require the scrap dealer to pay with a check, and to mail the check to a lockbox address, thereby removing all cash from the premises. Another option is to assume that a payment will be received from a scrap dealer on a relatively fixed schedule, and to make inquiries in the warehouse shortly after the expected scrap removal dates – thus notifying employees that management is watching.

Procurement Schemes

Procurement fraud involves any activity resulting in a business paying an excessive amount for goods or services. In some cases, a business may be conned into making a payment when no goods or services have been received at all. When procurement fraud is perpetrated over a long period of time, it can result in some of the largest fraud losses that an organization can experience. There are several types of procurement fraud, as noted in the following sub-sections.

Fake Invoice Fraud

A company may receive an invoice from a fake supplier, alleging that goods and services have been provided to the company. If the company does not do an adequate job of verifying these claims, it will pay the invoice. When a fake supplier finds that one of its invoices has been paid, it is more likely to continue sending invoices, probably for relatively low monetary amounts, so that these billings "fly under the radar" of the company's control systems. Thus, once successfully initiated, invoice fraud can last for a long time.

Invoice fraud can be limited by having a rigorous invoice approval process in place, preferably accompanied by a matching process that compares invoices to authorizing purchase orders and receiving reports.

The size of this fraud can be substantially greater when it is perpetrated by an employee. In this situation, the employee creates a shell company and enters it into his employer's accounting system as a valid supplier. This may be a state-registered company with a mailing address and usually its own bank account – thereby giving it an air of authenticity. The employee then creates dummy invoices and submits them to the company for approval. If the employee knows what the minimum cutoff level is within the company for invoice approvals, he can set the invoices at amounts just under this threshold, thereby escaping detection.

This type of fraud is quite difficult to detect if the amounts billed are kept low. If a person becomes bolder and submits larger invoices, then it will also be necessary for the person to override the invoice approval process, personally approve the invoices, or collude with an approved signer. This increased level of control over larger invoices makes it more difficult for anyone to sustain a large-dollar fraud with fake supplier billings. Nonetheless, the sheer volume of funds that can be stolen via fake suppliers continues to make this a popular fraud.

Diverted Purchases Fraud

A person working in the purchasing department can issue purchase orders to suppliers to deliver goods or services elsewhere and to charge the company. Since the purchasing person creates an authorizing purchase order, the resulting supplier invoices are usually paid without question. The diverted purchases are intended for the personal benefit of the employee. For example, goods could be delivered directly to the employee's home. This situation works especially well when the supplier in question is also delivering goods and services to the company; in this situation, the supplier is already established with the company and so is less likely to be investigated.

This type of fraud is quite difficult to spot, especially when the resulting expenses are buried in the cost of goods sold account (see the General Employee Fraud Observations topic at the end of this chapter).

Kickbacks

In a kickback scheme, a supplier pays a buyer a bribe in exchange for selecting the supplier to sell goods and services to the buyer's company. This results in inflated prices and/or substandard quality levels for the company. A variation on the concept is for the supplier to hire a relative of the purchasing agent, typically at an inflated level of compensation; by doing so, there is no traceable payment being made to the purchasing agent. Other variations are for the kickback recipient to take out a loan and have the loan payments paid by the supplier, or for the supplier to issue the person a credit card, with all payments on the card being made by the supplier.

This type of fraud can be found by comparing the prices paid to suppliers to the market price, to see if there is price inflation. This task is usually taken on by the internal audit department, which will probably only invest the investigation effort for larger purchasing contracts. Consequently, if the two conniving parties are careful, they can probably get away with smaller kickback schemes for a long time.

A less common variation on the kickback scheme is for a customer to pay the collections staff of a company in exchange for allowing their payments to extend longer than usual without designating the receivables as overdue (which might trigger an interest charge). There is a significant opportunity for fraud in this area when the amounts outstanding are quite large, and especially when there is a continuing series of invoices to be paid. This issue can be prevented to some extent by routinely shifting customer assignments among the collections staff, so that no one can take advantage of such a deal for long. The arrangement may also be detected by tracking the days outstanding for larger invoices.

Bid Rigging

A variation on the preceding kickback scheme is when an employee (usually a buyer in the purchasing department) assists a supplier in winning a competitive bid. Under a competitive bidding arrangement, a number of suppliers are asked to provide bids. A buyer can assist a preferred supplier by altering the terms of the bid solicitation to favor that supplier's goods and services, by informing the supplier of the terms of other bids already received, and by influencing the subsequent selection process to favor the indicated supplier. Another variation is to set up such a narrow time window within which to submit bids that most bidders are unable to submit bids on time, and so are rejected.

A bid rigging situation is not easily pinpointed, since the methods used may be so subtle that there is no clear indicator on an individual bid basis that anything is wrong. The situation is more obvious when a number of bids are aggregated, at which point it will become clear that a particular supplier is winning a disproportionate number of contracts.

Payables Schemes

Significant sums can be lost in the payables department, either due to fraud initiated by employees within this area, or because frauds originating elsewhere are not caught by the payables staff. We note several payables schemes in the following sub-sections.

Outbound Check Fraud

A company has been subjected to outbound check fraud when its checks have been stolen for use by the perpetrator. In this situation, the company will see checks being unexpectedly charged against its checking account.

An employee can steal blank check stock and use it to create checks payable to her. This is especially easy if the company keeps a signature stamp or signature plate in the same storage area as the check stock, so that breaking into just one cabinet gives the perpetrator all of the tools needed to engage in this kind of fraud. A variation is the concealed check scam, where a payables clerk creates a check made payable to herself or an associated entity, and slips it into a stack of checks to be signed by an authorized check signer. If the check signer has a reputation for signing anything without question, there is a good chance that the payables clerk will soon have a valid payment that can be cashed with impunity.

A variation on this concept is to intercept outgoing checks intended for suppliers, and modify them sufficiently to be able to deposit them into the individual's own account. The modification of an existing check can include forging the name of the payee and/or the amount paid. Doing so provides the person with a valid check that already has an authorized signature on it. Here are several variations on the concept:

- Intentionally pay a supplier twice and then demand that one of the checks be returned. The returned check is then intercepted and cashed.
- Intentionally pay the wrong supplier and then demand that the check be returned. The returned check is then intercepted and cashed.

Check theft is especially pernicious when the person engaging in the fraud is an authorized check signer, such as an in-charge bookkeeper or controller. This person has ready access to the check stock, and no one will question the checks being issued. The situation is especially bad if the person sets up fake suppliers, so that she can submit fake invoices, and is then authorized to issue the checks to pay for her own invoices.

Several controls can be used to prevent outbound check fraud. Unused check stock should be securely locked up when not in use, and a log should be maintained of all check numbers used. Also, the company should notify its bank of all check amounts it has issued (known as positive pay), so that the bank will only honor those checks when they are presented.

Diverted Payment Fraud

The payables clerk can prepare the same supplier invoice for approval twice. In the first pass, an adjustment is made to the "pay to" address, so that it is sent to an address controlled by the payables clerk or an accomplice. The check is then cashed, so that the clerk has access to the funds. Then, the clerk waits a few weeks and then submits a copy of the same invoice for approval, but now with the supplier's actual address listed as the "pay to" address. The supplier is paid on this second pass, so it will not call to complain about a late payment. This fraud can be made even more convincing if the payables clerk contacts the supplier, says that the original invoice appears to have been lost, and requests that a replacement invoice be sent. This approach results in a new invoice being submitted to the boss for approval, rather than a copy, which the manager is much less likely to delve into in any detail.

This fraud tends to arise in smaller companies, where there is just a bookkeeper and no one else in the accounting department, so it is difficult to impose enough oversight to spot the fraud. Instead, the best approach is detective in nature. Either the owner or an outside CPA can review the company's books to see if the supplier accounts used in this manner have any double payments.

Petty Cash Fraud

The administrator of a petty cash box can forge receipts for expenditures allegedly made from his petty cash fund, record the receipts, and steal the related amount of cash from the fund. A variation is to make copies of a receipt, alter the dates on the copies, and repeatedly submit them as reimbursed expenses over a period of time. Petty cash boxes usually contain modest amounts of cash, so the aggregate amount of cash stolen by this fraud is relatively small. Nonetheless, the controller should make it known that all petty cash receipts will be closely examined when petty cash boxes are to be replenished.

Expense Report Fraud

There are many ways in which an employee can file an expense report that contains false expenses. When reimbursed for these false claims, an employee is stealing funds. Here are multiple examples of the ways in which an expense report can be falsified:

General Issues

- *Multiple reimbursements.* An employee makes multiple copies of a receipt and continues to submit these extra receipts in successive expense reports, thereby being reimbursed several times for the same expenditure. A cleverer alternative is to submit several different types of support for the same expense in successive expense reports. For example, an employee could submit the itemized detail for a hotel room on one expense report and the credit card receipt for the room on the next report. A variation is to charge an item to the company credit card and then claim reimbursement for it on his expense report, using the transaction receipt.
- *Personal expenditures.* An employee includes various personal expenditures in an expense report. For example, a personal meal is characterized as a business lunch.
- *Adjusted receipts.* An employee deliberately alters a receipt to increase the amount to be reimbursed. If the alteration is visible, the person is more likely to submit a photocopy instead, on which the adjustment is less likely to be noticed.
- *Fake receipts.* An employee creates entirely fake documentation for a reimbursement claim, including an official-looking form, a fake company logo, and multiple line items that appear quite detailed and authentic.

Specific Situations

- *Educational reimbursement.* An employee submits a claim for expense reimbursement, using a receipt that shows he paid a college to enroll in a course. Once reimbursed, the employee cancels the class and is paid back by the college.
- *Meals reimbursement.* An employee is on an extended out-of-town consulting trip, and is reimbursed for all grocery store receipts, since he likes to cook his

own meals. When at the grocery store, he collects additional receipts from other people who have just gone through the checkout line, and submits these additional receipts for reimbursement.

- *Hotel reimbursement.* An employee buys meals at the hotel restaurant and has them charged to his room. He then submits a reimbursement request for the total hotel bill, while separately submitting a request for meal reimbursement.
- *Cab reimbursement.* An employee takes a cab ride, pays the driver in cash, and asks for a blank receipt, which he then fills out with a higher amount and submits for reimbursement.
- *Mileage reimbursement.* An employee overstates the amount of miles actually traveled on company business, in order to receive extra reimbursement.

In short, the amount of expense report padding is limited only by the inventiveness of employees. There are several possible prevention techniques to combat the situation. One is to flag certain employees for detailed expense report reviews, once any type of fraudulent claim is discovered on one of their reports (including an audit of their previous expense reports). Another option is to directly pay for as many travel expenses as possible. For example, a central travel group can pay for airlines and hotels. Further, charges can be made directly to a corporate expense card, thereby removing charged items from the employee expense report. Ideally, the outcome should be quite small or even nonexistent expense reports.

Human Resources Schemes

A large part of the expenditures of a business are related to its employees, so it should be no surprise that there are a multitude of methods that employees have derived to illicitly extract cash from this area, or simply to gain employment. The following subtopics cover the full range of human resources activities, including job applications, compensation, benefits administration, and time reporting.

Job Application Fraud

A common form of fraud occurs when job applicants overstate their qualifications when applying for a job. By doing so, a business is more likely to hire people who are unqualified for jobs, resulting in the payment of excessively high compensation and/or inferior work by these individuals. Job application fraud is pervasive, and should be considered to be present to some degree in most applications. Consequently, it is essential for the personnel department to spend an adequate amount of time verifying the information presented by each job applicant who is considered to be a finalist for a position.

Compensation Fraud

There are multiple ways in which employees can falsely obtain payment for compensation that they have not earned. For example, any hourly wage earner can submit a timesheet with overtime hours stated that he or she did not actually work. If there is no control in place for formally approving these hours, the overtime may be paid with no review at all. Or, if an employee claims just a minor amount of overtime on an ongoing basis, this could pass beneath the attention of a supervisor, who allows the payment to be made.

There are several ways for a payroll clerk to engage in compensation fraud. Consider the following possibilities:

- *Alter hours*. No matter how many hours were approved by supervisors, a payroll clerk can still enter a different number of hours into the payroll system. The recipient could then kick back some of the difference to the clerk, as compensation.
- *Alter rate*. The payroll clerk can alter the pay rate paid to one or more employees. The recipients kick back some of the difference to the clerk, as compensation.
- *Alter commission*. The compensation of a salesperson can be enhanced by artificially increasing the amount of sales credited to the person, so that a larger commission is paid. Alternatively, a payroll clerk can inflate the commission rate paid to a sales person.
- *Use ghost employees*. When an employee leaves the company, a payroll clerk continues to pay the person for a few additional pay periods, and changes the direct deposit information to route money into his or her bank account. At a more egregious level, these ghost employees can be maintained in the system for long periods of time.

All of these types of compensation fraud can be prevented by installing controls. There should be supervisory authorization of all overtime, cross-checking of hours paid against the authorizing timesheets, verification of pay rates against authorized pay levels, and matching of official employee lists against the payroll register. In addition, there should be an automated log that records all changes to the pay rates posted in the payroll database.

A separate issue involving compensation fraud occurs when a salesperson triggers the creation of a fake invoice in order to meet a periodic sales quota, which usually causes a bonus to be paid. After the bonus has been paid, the salesperson can fudge the situation by saying that the customer has withdrawn its purchase order or wants to combine the amounts stated on the invoice into another order that has not yet been issued. This type of fraud can be minimized by insisting on the receipt of formal, signed customer purchase orders before any invoices will be issued.

Dependent Fraud

A business may find that employees are classifying other people as dependents in order to obtain benefits for them. A common example is that a child is now too old to qualify as a dependent, but the parent does not notify the employer that the person should be removed from benefit coverage. The employer continues to pay for coverage. Benefit fraud is more of a concern in organizations with thousands of employees, where there is a large pool of dependents to be monitored.

Benefit fraud can be detected by engaging in a rolling audit of all covered employees, to spot instances of excess coverage.

Workers' Compensation Fraud

An employee can fake having incurred an injury while on the job, and files a workers' compensation claim. He then receives compensation while recuperating from the "injury". Though the cost of these claims is initially borne by the insurer, the insurance premium charged to the employer will rise, so that the fake claim will eventually become an expense of the employer. An especially pernicious version of workers' compensation fraud is when the employee is in cahoots with a doctor, who files fake medical treatment claims and then splits the proceeds with the employee.

This type of fraud is most apparent when the circumstances of a claim are suspicious (such as someone allegedly slipping on the floor in a completely dry (and distant) part of the warehouse, or when there is an ongoing pattern of claims.

Self-Insurance Fraud

A business may self-insure its medical insurance. This usually involves directly paying for smaller claims, with catastrophic coverage by an outside insurer for larger claims. In this situation, doctors are supposed to submit claims directly to the company for reimbursement. An employee in the claims department can take advantage of this arrangement by creating several fake doctors, and forwarding fake claims from them to the company's claims department. The individual can then approve the claims for payment. The payables department then issues payments to the mailing addresses of the fake doctors, which the employee collects.

An independent review of claims, along with an examination of the existence of the doctors submitting claims, is the best way to detect this type of fraud. It may also be worthwhile to see if the mailing addresses of any doctors are the same, or if these addresses match the mailing addresses of any employees.

Time Fraud

An employer is subject to the loss of employee time when employees mis-represent their activities; they state that they are working on company business when they are instead occupied with non-work activities. Since the company is paying their compensation, this constitutes theft of wages. For example, an employee takes advantage of a flexible-hours arrangement to start work late and leave early, resulting in a shorter-than-normal work day. Or, the person calls in sick and then spends the time working elsewhere.

Time fraud is a particular concern in cases where a person is needed for the full duration of the work day, as may be the case for a customer service person that needs to be available to take customer calls. It is less of an issue when employees are being paid to accomplish certain objectives; as long as the objectives are met, a reasonable case can be made that time fraud is not occurring.

There are several ways to mitigate the effects of time fraud. For example, the option of using flexible work hours can be limited to the most reliable employees and rolled out slowly to additional personnel, depending on how successive tranches of employees deal with this arrangement. Another possibility is to require clocking in and out for an expanded group of employees, in order to collect evidence that they are on the premises (particularly effective when biometric timeclocks are used). A less intrusive approach is to rely on feedback from employees to determine who is taking advantage of the company, and then assign the applicable managers to more closely monitor the highlighted individuals.

Executive-Level Fraud

Some types of employee fraud are most likely perpetrated by members of the executive team, since they are in a position to authorize certain types of transactions that are not available to other employees. These activities include the authorization of loans, insider trading, and stock option backdating, as addressed in the following sub-sections.

Abuse of a Position of Trust

The abuse of a position of trust occurs when a person uses his position of authority or trust for personal gain, at the expense of a third party. For example, a company president gives a trusted attorney access to the company's wire transfer passwords, which the attorney then uses to shift company funds out of the country. As another example, a person is a trustee of a company's pension fund, and misdirects money from the fund for his own personal gain.

There are several possible indicators of this type of fraud. One indicator is when a person given sole control over assets resists efforts to appoint additional trustees. In this situation, the person realizes that other trustees are more likely to discover that assets have been stolen. Another indicator is when a person tries to keep certain transactions secret from other trustees. For example, an attorney given access to a company's bank accounts persuades the company president to not reveal the existence of this access to other members of the management team. A more generic indicator of fraud is when the person in the position of trust suddenly exhibits a significant increase in his spending behavior.

An essential curb on this type of fraud is to require those in a position of trust to make joint decisions. This means that several people must decide to take action, rather than giving this power to a single individual. Doing so does not eliminate the risk of fraud, but makes it less likely, since several people would need to act together (collusion) in order to misdirect assets.

Executive and Related Party Loan Fraud

Corporate executives may authorize that loans be made by the company to themselves or to family, friends, or businesses operated by these individuals. These loans typically have unusually favorable terms, and may even be forgiven at a later date. In effect, these are cash handouts to the benefiting executives and related parties. The amounts paid out through this type of fraud can be substantial, since management is directly approving the issuance of funds – there is no attempt to hide the transfer of cash.

Loans to members of management or outside parties should be approved in advance by the board of directors. However, executives can use their authority within the organization to override this requirement, so that the board never knows that loans have been granted or forgiven. Given the participation of senior managers in this scam, it can be difficult to develop any type of valid control for it, since the managers can override the controls.

Insider Trading Fraud

Insider trading occurs when employees have knowledge of information that is not yet available to the public, and use this information to buy or sell company securities at advantageous prices. For example, the CFO of a business knows that reported sales levels will decline in the next quarterly financial statements, so he sells his shares in the company in advance of the information release. The CFO avoids a loss in the market value of his shares by timing the sale of the shares.

Insider trading does not harm the company, but most definitely harms its investors, since they may be buying securities from or selling securities to people who have better knowledge of what those securities are really worth.

There are significant insider trading legal penalties, which are classified as felonies; all insiders who hold company stock can be regularly advised of the penalties associated with insider trading.

Stock Option Backdating Fraud

Stock options give their holder the right to purchase the common stock of a corporation at a specific price. This right is available over a date range, such as for the next five years. Once a stock option is used to buy shares, these shares are typically sold right away, in order to pay any related income taxes. Consequently, a person who has been awarded stock options will only use them if the current market price is higher than the exercise price built into the options. The exercise price is usually the market price of the shares on the date when the options were awarded. For example, a person is awarded 1,000 stock options that allow him to buy the shares of the employer for $10.00 per share. After three years have passed, the price of the shares has increased to $12.00. The investor exercises the options to buy 1,000 shares from his employer for $10,000. He immediately sells the shares on the open market for $12,000, pocketing a profit of $2,000.

An issue with stock options that management can illegally take advantage of is to backdate the options. The date at which the option price is set is shifted backward to that date on which the market price of the stock was the lowest. By doing so, those awarded stock options can now buy the shares at a lower exercise price, so that they reap larger profits when they sell the shares. To use a variation on the preceding example, management backdates the stock options by three weeks, to a day on which the company's stock price was $9.00 per share. The person awarded the options later buys the shares at $9.00 and sells them for $12,000, resulting in a profit of $3,000.

Because of the backdating, the individual earned a 50% larger profit than would otherwise have been the case.

This type of fraud is difficult to spot, since it is not immediately apparent in a company's financial statements. Instead, one must examine the date of the board of directors meeting minutes to see when the options were authorized, and then trace this date back to when the options documentation was completed. A disparity between the dates indicates that backdating has occurred.

General Employee Fraud Observations

We have already noted a variety of fraud mitigation techniques within the preceding discussions of individual fraud schemes. At a more general level, there are a number of mitigation activities that can be used to minimize fraud by employees. They are:

General Prevention

- The management team exhibits stringent adherence to company ethics, thereby setting an example for employees.
- Have a whistleblowing policy with a rewards system that encourages employees to forward fraud information to management.
- Publicize a zero tolerance policy toward any type of employee fraud.
- Prosecute those found to have engaged in fraud, to set an example.

Employee Focus

- Thoroughly examine the background of prospective employees before hiring them.

Facility Focus

- Tightly control access to the building with an employee identification system.
- Lock up critical information in secure areas.

Process Focus

- Ensure that there is a segregation of duties where the handling of assets is involved, so that more than one person is engaged in tasks.
- Require varying levels of expenditure approvals, so that large payments have been authorized by several people.
- Reconcile accounts regularly and investigate any anomalies found.
- Periodically audit processes throughout the business.
- Directly pay for all expenditures, rather than routing payments through employee expense reports.

An excellent place in which to search for problematic transactions is the cost of goods sold account. A large number of transactions flow through this account every year. Also, since the account balance is zeroed out at the end of the fiscal year, any entries made to the account are eliminated at year-end. Given these characteristics of the account, it should be no surprise that the canny employee will record fraud-related transactions in the cost of goods sold account. Since the aggregate expense recorded in this account is so large, an individual could hide quite a large embezzlement arrangement here and have an excellent chance of never being caught.

Summary

A continuing theme in this chapter has been the need to segregate duties among different employees, so that no one individual has complete responsibility for a process (such as cash receipts). This presents a problem for smaller organizations, where there may be just one person in the accounting department, one person in the warehouse, and so forth. In these instances, the owners may need to take on the added role of conducting periodic reviews of company processes, to see if there are any unexplained transactions occurring. Fraud becomes less of an issue as the company headcount increases, since the segregation of duties is presumably being enforced. However, new risks appear in a larger organization. One is that continuing growth of the business can result in weak control points where new processes have been installed without conducting a thoughtful review of controls. Employees may take advantage of these weak spots to remove company assets. Also, a larger firm has so many assets that the management team may find that it can readily override company controls to siphon off a substantial amount of assets. In short, there is always a danger of fraud from employees, no matter what size a business may be.

Chapter 2
Financial Statement Fraud Schemes

Introduction

There are always new cases being publicized in which companies falsify their financial statements. Why would anyone do this? There are many reasons that can strongly motivate people to falsely adjust financial statements. Consider the following:

- *Bonuses.* A management team is presented with an aggressive bonus package under which they receive massive payouts, but only if they attain stretch goals for financial performance. This is a strong incentive for the management team to connive to adjust the stated financial results in order to trigger their bonus payments. The situation is even more likely to result in fraud if the bulk of management compensation is skewed toward bonuses.
- *Covenants.* There may be covenants associated with a loan that allow the lender to call the loan if the business no longer displays certain performance or liquidity metrics. If the loan is called, the business may fail. This situation also presents a powerful motivation to adjust the financials to ensure that the covenant thresholds are surpassed.
- *Investor expectations.* A publicly-held business is under constant pressure from investors to continually report better results. This is especially the case if there are threats from investors to take over the board of directors and then oust the management team. In essence, the management team is tempted to manage the stock price, rather than just running the business and letting the stock price fall where it may. This situation also routinely results in financial statement fraud.
- *Loan guarantees.* In a closely-owned business, some members of management may have personally guaranteed the company's debt. If so, these individuals could see their personal savings and assets wiped out if the business fails. This prospect gives them a major incentive to report adequate financial results for the business.
- *Ownership impact.* Many managers have large stock holdings in their businesses. If the share price were to fall, these people would suffer substantial losses in their investment portfolios. Consequently, they prop up reported earnings to keep the stock price high.
- *Stock options.* The management team may have a substantial number of stock options, and will benefit from exercising the options at a high stock price. Therefore, they have an incentive to enhance the results of the business during the dates when they can exercise their stock options.
- *Tax concerns.* In a business where earnings flow through to a small group of owners, there is a reverse incentive to report the *smallest* possible amount of

taxable income, so that tax payments are minimized. This can result in efforts to minimize or defer reported revenues, while maximizing or accelerating the recognition of expenses.

- *Temporary shortfalls.* A business may suffer what appears to be a temporary shortfall in revenues or profits, so management covers the shortfall by adjusting the books. Then, when the shortfall turns out not to be temporary, the shifting of revenues and other adjustments leaves a gaping hole in the financial statements in later periods, which must then be covered up with further financial trickery. In essence, a small adjustment gradually builds into a major accounting fraud.

A key factor underlying several of the preceding points is that there is a significant value associated with presenting sales and earnings that continue to increase at a smooth pace. When there are no unexpected spikes or dips in these growth rates, investors assume that a business has a lower risk of failure, and so will bid its stock price higher. This means that managers are motivated to present a steady and predictable rate of increase, which may diverge quite a bit from what is actually happening.

In this chapter, we describe a multitude of ways to falsify financial statements. Please note that many of these techniques require the active connivance of at least some of the management team; it would be quite difficult for the company controller to make a broad range of fraudulent adjustments without the approval of other managers.

Sales Inflation

The managers of a business might try to falsely increase sales. Their intent could be to cover a shortfall in projected sales for a short period of time, or perhaps to artificially bolster sales over a longer period. Here are several options they might attempt to use:

- *Accelerate recognition on mixed sale arrangements.* When a company sells a mix of goods and services, it overstates the price of the goods (which can be recognized at once), while underpricing the price of the services (which are recognized over a longer period of time).
- *Bill and hold transactions.* Under these arrangements, the seller recognizes revenue while retaining the goods that should have been shipped to the customer, allegedly because the customer wants the seller to store the goods on the customer's behalf. The seller may forge documents, stating that the customer has authorized this arrangement.
- *Billing of cost overruns.* Under several types of construction reimbursement contracts, the buyer compensates the seller for cost overruns – but only after the customer approves a formal change order. If the seller were to record these cost overruns as revenue prior to a change order, it would constitute falsification of revenues.

- *Combine a business unit sale with guaranteed future product sales.* A company may choose to sell off one of its business units. In order to falsely generate more sales in future periods, the transaction is structured to sell the unit at an artificially low price, while requiring the buyer to purchase goods from the parent company for a certain period of time and at an inflated price. The net effect of the deal is that the parent company converts a one-time gain on the sale of its subsidiary into operating revenue that it can recognize in the future.
- *Consignment sales.* A business sends goods to a third party, which has agreed to sell the goods to the ultimate buyer on behalf of the company. Under a consignment arrangement, there is no sale until delivery is made to the ultimate buyer. When the business records a sale at the point when it delivers goods to the consignee, this is a fraudulent acceleration of the related sale.
- *Create fake invoices.* One of the more egregious ways to boost sales is to create fake invoices in order to boost sales. A clever perpetrator will create invoices of relatively small size that are unlikely to be audited, or invoices to foreign firms that the auditors may consider to be too difficult to confirm through their auditing activities.
- *Create revenue journal entries.* Management can simply create a journal entry that credits sales and debits accounts receivable, thereby instantly generating sales even when there is no underlying transaction at all. This is called a *topside entry*, for it is made to the general ledger, not to any supporting subledgers. Topside entries are a favorite tool for falsely adjusting revenue, because they do not require collusion with other departments; management simply makes its own entries.
- *Delay recordation of discounts.* When discounts are granted to customers on sales transactions, the amount eventually collected from the customers will be reduced, which means that the initial sales figure should be reduced by the amount of these discounts. Delaying the recordation of sales discounts into a later period will result in a temporary boost in the sales figure. One way to systematize this concept is to bill customers at the full list price and then deduct any discounts only when recording cash received from the customers.
- *Delay recordation of returns.* When goods are returned by customers, this is recorded as a reduction of sales. When management wants to keep sales as high as possible in the current period, they delay the recordation of sales returns until a later period.
- *Gross up revenue.* An entity that acts as an agent for another party should only recognize as revenue the commission it earns on a sale, not the entire amount of the sale. An organization can use various pretexts under the accounting rules to claim that it can actually recognize all of these types of sales. For example, an airline ticket broker may claim the entire amount of a sold ticket as revenue, when it should really be just the amount of the commission earned on the deal.
- *Keep the period open.* The end of the reporting period is allowed to stay open into the following day (or in egregious cases, for several days), so that

shipments occurring on the next day are recorded as sales in the previous reporting period.

- *Manipulate the percentage of completion.* When there are lengthy projects associated with revenues (such as the construction of a building), revenue is recognized based on the estimated percentage of completion. Thus, a 50% completion rate means that 50% of the contract revenue can be recognized. Sales can be inflated simply by increasing the assumed percentage of completion.

- *Misclassify sales.* A one-time gain on an asset sale is mis-classified as being part of revenues. Another variation is to classify investment income as sales.

- *Pipeline stuffing.* A business could encourage its customers, retailers, and distributors to accept additional products in order to achieve a short-term boost in sales. This may be accomplished by offering to take back unused goods, offering long-term payment terms, or large discounts from the normal list price. The intent behind doing so is to create a burst of sales that will be misconstrued by the readers of the entity's financial statements as an increase in long-term sales.

- *Recognize sales on incomplete orders.* There may be customer orders in process that have not been completed as of the end of the reporting period, so managers authorize these orders to be recognized as complete. A variation on the concept is to recognize sales prior to customer approval; this typically occurs when there is a lengthy product installation process.

- *Related-party sales.* A company sells assets to an entity that is controlled by the corporate parent or a common investor, resulting in a gain. However, since the ownership of both entities is the same, it is really an intercompany transaction that should have been backed out of the financial statements.

- *Round-tripping.* An organization sells certain assets to another party, promising to buy them back at a later date. Doing so creates revenue, though there is no economic justification for the continual shifting of assets back and forth. The more elaborate forms of this arrangement may even involve three parties, so that the nature of the activity is more obscure and difficult to detect.

- *Ship excess inventory.* A company ships extra goods to customers and bills them for the excess. The intent behind doing so is to book additional sales. Some customers may accept the extra merchandise, though most can be expected to return the goods after the end of the reporting period. The result for the company is a spike in sales, followed by a sharp decline when the sales returns are booked.

- *Ship goods early.* A customer may only want to have goods delivered as of a certain date, perhaps because it is operating a just-in-time system, and there is no room for the on-site storage of early deliveries. The company may ship early in order to record the sale within the reporting period, though there is a risk of annoying the customer.

- *Ship to company-owned warehouse.* A business can ostensibly ship goods and recognize the revenue associated with those goods, while actually just sending the goods to a warehouse that is owned by the company. The warehouse is essentially a way-point for goods that allows a business to recognize sales early, holding the goods for a short time and then forwarding them to the ultimate customer.

- *Side agreements.* A company can enter into undocumented side agreements with its customers that grant the customers special rights, such as the right to send back goods for an inordinately long time. Because these agreements are not documented, there is no proof that sales are being recorded sooner than should really be the case.

If the intent is to artificially increase sales for a long period of time, the fraud involves the creation of entirely new customer orders. This can include fake customer purchase orders, with a fake set of supporting documents to show how the orders were handled within the company and fulfilled.

Expenses Falsification

The preceding list of falsifications related to sales was enormous. The list of possibilities for adjusting expenses is quite a bit smaller, but can still have a significant impact on reported profit levels. The key expense falsifications are:

- *Capitalize expenses.* A business can recognize expenses as assets, thereby deferring expense recognition until a later period. These expenses are usually parked in one or more fixed asset accounts, but can be stored in a number of imaginatively-named asset accounts. Certain types of expenses are more likely to be incorrectly capitalized, such as advertising and other marketing costs, where the argument is that marketing expenditures are a cost of attracting new customers. Under this logic, the costs are then charged to expense over the period of time that the company expects to have the customers. A business may also attempt to capitalize a large part of its start-up costs.
- *Slow the amortization rate.* When expenditures have been capitalized, management can further slow the rate of their conversion to expenses by slowing down the rate of amortization. Amortization is the process of charging assets off to expense. For example, marketing costs are capitalized into a customer acquisition asset, and management then decides that the amortization rate will be 10 years. Doing so spreads the expense recognition over quite a long period of time and keeps profit levels unusually high in the interim. Management can alter all types of asset amortization periods, including depreciation rates for fixed assets, in order to defer expense recognition.
- *Do not record invoices.* Management holds supplier invoices until the following reporting period, and then allows the accounts payable staff to record them in the accounting system. Doing so shifts the expense out of the current period and into the next one. This approach is typically only used for a few larger invoices, to make the practice less obvious to auditors.

- *Do not accrue expenses.* Management may skip the accrual of various expenses, such as accrued wages, bonuses, commissions, and so forth. By doing so, the related expense recognition is shifted into the following period.
- *Avoid loss reserves.* A prudent business will record loss reserves for warranty claims, lawsuit payouts, and so forth. A management team that is intent on minimizing reported expense levels will avoid creating any of these reserves. Instead, they only recognize expenses as they actually occur, which could be at a later date.
- *Reduce loss reserves.* When there are existing loss reserves, management reverses some or all of the amounts in them, thereby reporting a negative expense in the income statement. A more conniving management team will establish one or more generic loss reserve accounts, and shift expenses into and out of them in order to manage the earnings level from period to period.

Marketable Securities Falsification

A business is supposed to record its marketable securities at their market values as of the ending date of each reporting period. The market value is derived from the reported prices at which securities sell. This might initially appear to be an area in which little fraud is possible, since the calculation is based on publicly-available information. However, the securities of many public companies are not traded on formal exchanges. Instead, they are listed on the over-the-counter market, where trading is much thinner. In these cases, a company could bid up the price of a stock just before month-end with just a few small purchases, and then value all of its holdings in that stock at the month-end value. The falsification is only apparent when looking at the trend line of prices for the stock on a daily basis.

Prepaid Expenses Falsification

The prepaid expenses account is supposed to contain expenditures that have been paid for in one accounting period, but for which the underlying asset will not be entirely consumed until a future period. An example of a prepaid expense is insurance, which is frequently paid in advance for multiple future periods; an entity initially records this expenditure as a prepaid expense, and then charges it to expense over the usage period.

When a company wants to make its financial results look better, it overloads the prepaid expenses account by adding expenses that should have been charged to expense at once. Instead, these expenses are recognized in a future period. The alteration of this account is typically used to make smaller adjustments to the financial statements on a short-term basis, where the intent is to clean up the account shortly thereafter.

Receivables Falsification

There are multiple ways to falsify an organization's accounts receivable. In the following points, we outline several of the more common ones. They are:

- *Date alteration.* When a business engages in suspect sales activities, the related accounts receivables will eventually age to the point where they are clearly overdue for payment, and should be written off (thereby causing a loss). To prevent a write-off, the accounting staff alters the dates on the invoices or credits the invoices to eliminate them, and replaces them with debit memos or invoices that have a more current date.
- *Minimize reserves.* A relatively common financial statement adjustment is to maintain an excessively low allowance for doubtful accounts. When this happens, the allowance does not accurately reflect the amount of bad debt that is contained within accounts receivable. The result is that bad debts are more likely to be charged to expense in a later period, when specific invoices are written off. This means that the current period profit is overstated by the understatement of this allowance.
- *Delay bad debt recognition.* A variation on the last concept is to delay recognizing bad debts until a later period. When a bad debt is recognized, it is written off by offsetting it against the allowance for doubtful accounts. By delaying this recognition, the allowance looks bigger than it really is, making it appear that no additional charge to bad debts expense is needed.
- *Offload questionable receivables.* When it appears that some receivables will not be collected, the company sells them to another entity, usually at full value. The buying entity could be controlled by a related party, so that the sale is a sham.
- *Shift to notes receivable.* A company can convince some of its customers to sign paperwork that converts trade receivables into notes receivable. By doing so, the company can remove these items from its accounts receivable line item, thereby producing a misleading comparison of sales to receivables, indicating that receivables are more current than is really the case.

Loss Reserves Falsification

A business could record a large loss reserve, taking a massive charge against earnings in one period. The argument favoring the use of this reserve is that the business is about to discontinue some of its operations, engage in a restructuring, complete an environmental cleanup, and so forth, and wants to recognize all related losses at once. As expenditures are incurred in later periods, they are charged against the reserve, for which the expense was already recognized.

This is fine, except when the amount of the loss is overstated. When there is too much of a loss, the reserve turns into a bank that can be reversed whenever needed to offset operating expenses, resulting in incorrectly high profits. For example, a business recognizes a $1,000,000 charge against earnings that relates to the forthcoming shuttering of its widget production facility. However, management knows that the actual amount of these losses will be much closer to $300,000, leaving a reserve of $700,000 that is available for other uses. A few periods later, the company records an inordinately high legal expense, so the controller is instructed to debit the reserve by $60,000 and credit the legal expense in the same amount, resulting in a reduction in the reported legal expense.

The use of excessive loss reserves is particularly common in the following circumstances:

- *New team.* A new management team has been hired to replace a poorly-performing team, and sets up a loss reserve right away, under the guise of needing to write off any number of things to clean up the mess. Actually, the loss is then used to manage earnings for the next few accounting periods in order to show gradual improvement in reported results.
- *Excess earnings.* Earnings are already quite good, but management foresees that earnings could begin to decline, so it writes off a large amount into a loss reserve under a pretext. The reserve is then used to bolster subsequent earnings.
- *Losses add-on.* A company is already suffering massive losses and a large decline in its stock price. Management presumes that adding on more losses at this point will make little difference, so it adds on a loss reserve, which can be used to manage earnings in the future.

The use of loss reserves can be detected by keeping track of the loss reserve balance on the balance sheet. As it gradually declines over time, inquire as to how the reserve was used.

Inventory Falsification

When the ending valuation of inventory is adjusted, this has a direct impact on the reported amount of income. The reason is that the cost of goods sold is calculated using the following formula:

$$\text{Beginning inventory} + \text{Purchases} - \text{Ending inventory} = \text{Cost of goods sold}$$

Thus, if the amount of ending inventory is artificially increased, this reduces the cost of goods sold, which increases profits. Given this effect, it should be no surprise that multiple scams have been originated to modify ending inventory, including the following:

- *Claim consigned inventory.* When a business holds consigned inventory on behalf of a consignor, it does not own the inventory. One can easily count these items and include them in ending inventory in order to inflate inventory levels.
- *Delay purchase recordation.* When purchases are recorded, they form the middle part of the cost of goods sold calculation that was just described. Thus,

if someone wants to report a lower cost of goods sold, the entry of a supplier's invoice is just delayed until the following reporting period. Of course, this will then increase the cost of goods sold in the next reporting period.

- *Delay shrinkage charges.* The inventory may shrink for any number of reasons, including theft, damage, and inventory items exceeding their usage dates. These items should be promptly subtracted from inventory, which reduces profits. If the management team simply refuses to authorize the shrinkage charges, then inventory will be overstated.
- *Double counting.* Two separate count teams could be routed to the same inventory area at different times, resulting in each team innocently counting the same inventory. Doing so doubles the ending inventory count for the targeted items.
- *Inflate overhead.* Factory overhead is allocated to ending inventory, and can form a substantial part of the total inventory balance at month-end. This amount can be manipulated by altering the accounts that are included in factory overhead, or by altering the allocation methodology.
- *Mis-calculate inventory extensions.* The computer program used to multiply ending unit counts by costs per unit can be programmed to yield inflated figures. Or, if an electronic spreadsheet is used, a selection of manual overrides can be made to achieve the same result.
- *Move inventory.* Management can arrange to have inventory counted at one location on one day, and then moved to another location and counted again the next day. This scam requires that counts be staggered across several days.
- *Overstate the percentage of completion of work-in-process.* When goods have not yet been completed by the end of a reporting period, a cost is assigned to them based on their percentage of completion. When this percentage is artificially raised, so too is the inventory valuation.
- *Recognize fictitious inventory.* Someone could record entirely fake inventory, along with supporting purchase and storage documents. This approach works best when there are no scheduled inventory counts in the near future, so that there is no risk of someone spotting these items.
- *Repackage scrap inventory.* Inventory items designated as scrap or rework can be packaged into finished goods boxes at month-end and counted as normal finished goods.
- *Use incorrect costs.* When an inventory count is conducted at the end of a reporting period, the units on hand are supposed to be multiplied by the relevant unit cost, depending on the cost flow assumptions being used by the business (such as the first in, first out method). One could replace a selection of these costs with an adjusted amount, thereby altering the amount of ending inventory.

Inventory-related fraud tends to be used to manufacture artificial results for just a short period of time, since modifications to ending inventory balances are self-correcting. This is because the modified ending inventory balance for one period becomes the beginning inventory balance for the *next* period. Therefore, if someone does not continually alter the ending inventory balance in each consecutive month, the false reporting will be automatically flushed out of the system.

Fixed Asset Falsification

There are several ways to shift expenses into a later period by altering the fixed assets accounts, thereby increasing profits in the current period. These adjustments are as follows:

- *Allocate purchase costs to land.* The land asset is not depreciated. The ramification from a fraud perspective is that, when a grouping of land and buildings is acquired as part of a single deal, as much of the purchase price as possible should be allocated to the land portion of the deal. The result is that a large part of the purchase is never depreciated.
- *Capitalize compensation costs.* Management could capitalize an excessive amount of labor costs into the costs of fixed assets. This is especially common for constructed assets, where there is a better justification for doing so.
- *Create fake assets.* A business could report fixed assets that have no basis in reality. The assets may simply be added to the books, perhaps with an offset to an equity account. Doing so appears to increase the amount of assets that can be used as collateral for loans, while also increasing equity, which makes the organization appear more financially stable.
- *Create intangible assets.* Management could capitalize a variety of operating expenses as fixed assets, thereby deferring recognition of the related expense. For example, software development costs could be capitalized into the cost of software, as well as research & development costs and start-up costs. The accounting standards limit the circumstances under which operating costs can be capitalized, so this approach requires some aggressive stretching of the rules.
- *Increase useful lives.* The assumed useful lives of fixed assets can be increased, thereby spreading depreciation expense over a longer period of time. Useful lives may be extended for just the largest fixed assets, thereby making this alteration more difficult to spot while still maximizing the amount of depreciation expense that is deferred into future periods.
- *Increase salvage values.* Salvage values are assigned to fixed assets that do not currently have one, and existing salvage values are increased. By doing so, the amount of depreciation that will be charged against fixed assets is reduced. This approach is less easy to detect when only a few assets are assigned salvage values.
- *Increase interest capitalization.* The accounting staff liberally interprets the rules for assigning interest costs to long-term fixed asset projects, so that more interest costs are assigned to these projects, rather than being charged to expense as incurred.

- *Lower capitalization threshold.* The cutoff point at which expenditures are recorded as fixed assets is dropped, so that more expenses are converted into fixed assets. This spreads the recognition of expenses over several years.
- *Avoid asset write-offs.* When an asset is impaired, the amount of the impairment is supposed to be charged to expense at once. This is a particular issue with the goodwill derived from acquisitions; many organizations find that their goodwill balances must be written down. Management could mandate that all impairments are to be ignored. This also involves misleading the auditors, who will make inquiries about whether any asset impairments exist.

Liability Falsification

When a business does not record liabilities, the associated expenses are not recorded, thereby leading to increased profits. The following scams are used to achieve a lower level of liabilities:

- *Reduced accruals.* When an asset is consumed, there should be a related expense in the same period. When there is no associated supplier invoice for a period of time, the accounting staff is supposed to record an expense accrual. When this does not happen, the expense is shifted into a later period, when the invoice eventually arrives. This can be a particular problem with property taxes, since the bill is only sent once a year. Other types of accruals that may be ignored or understated are:
  - o Insurance payable
  - o Interest payable
  - o Payroll taxes payable
  - o Pension payments payable
  - o Rent payable
  - o Utilities payable
  - o Vacations payable
  - o Wages payable
- *Recognizing self-insurance as incurred.* When a business self-insures, the accounting staff could incorrectly defer expense recognition by waiting until claims are actually received, which could be months or even years later.
- *Delayed recordation.* When a large supplier invoice arrives near month-end, it is withheld from the accounting system and only recorded in the following month after the current month has closed. This effectively shifts the expense into the next reporting period.
- *Inflate purchase returns.* The amount of returns to suppliers can be inflated, which creates credits that offset the amounts owed to suppliers. This scam is especially pernicious, because it can originate in the shipping department rather than the accounting department. Someone in shipping forges product return documentation and sends it to accounting, so that the accounting staff thinks the returns are valid.

- *Inflate purchase discounts.* A company may claim to qualify for purchase discounts, such as volume discounts that are calculated following the end of each year. These discounts can be accrued even in the absence of actual credits being issued by suppliers.
- *Avoid setting up a warranty reserve.* A business might have a number of ongoing warranty claims from customers, in which case it should set up a warranty reserve when sales are initially generated, so that the related warranty expense is recognized at once. When there is no warranty reserve, the related warranty expense is only recognized when an actual customer claim is received, which could be months later.
- *Record deposits as revenue.* When a customer pays a deposit on an order, this amount is supposed to be recorded as a liability until such time as the related product or service has been shipped or completed, respectively. At that time, the deposit liability is eliminated and a sale is recorded. The accounting department could instead record these deposits as revenue right away, thereby understating liabilities. A more aggressive form of this fraud is when a deposit is supposed to be returned to a customer at a later date, as occurs when a renter makes a deposit that is to be paid back when the lease term expires. A company could record this type of deposit as revenue; doing so manufactures revenue that does not actually exist.
- *Use aggressive pension assumptions.* In a defined benefit pension plan, employees are guaranteed certain benefits. This type of plan calls for constant, ongoing accounting adjustments by the employer over the life of the plan, based on estimates of how much will be earned on invested pension funds and various assumptions regarding benefit usage levels and the death rates of participants. A business can use aggressive assumptions when calculating its pension obligation, such as assuming that an unusually high return will be generated on invested funds.
- *Waffle on contingent liabilities.* A contingent liability is supposed to be recorded when it is probable that the loss will occur, and it is reasonably possible to estimate the amount of the loss. A company can waffle on recording these liabilities by either ignoring them or by understating the probable amount of the liability. If it is reasonably possible that a contingent liability will occur, the liability should be disclosed in the accompanying footnotes to the financial statements. Again, management could choose to ignore these liabilities, not reporting them in the disclosures at all.

Debt Falsification

There are several ways in which to alter the amount of debt liability that a business is recording in its financial statements. Consider the following types of fraud:

- *Misrepresentation of debt.* A relatively common occurrence is for the owner of a closely-held business to contribute funds to the organization, and to characterize it as equity. By doing so, the business appears to be more stable, with a lower ratio of debt to equity. However, the owner's real intent is that the contribution is a loan, for which there is an expectation of repayment, along with interest. This situation may not become apparent until a later date, when the owner alters the underlying documents to shift the equity payment into a debt payment.

- *Not recording loans.* The owners of a business may take out loans that are collateralized by company assets, and retain the proceeds from the loans. These arrangements are not stated in the financial statements of the company, even though they are liabilities of the company.
- *Claiming forgiveness of debt.* Management can claim that a debt was forgiven by a lender, either in whole or in part. Not only does this eliminate a potentially major liability, it also creates a gain on the forgiveness of debt, which bolsters profits. This situation can appear to be correct in substance, especially when the debt is unsecured and the company refuses to pay the lender; in effect, the loan will not be paid, so the question is whether the loan is in default or has been forgiven.

Discontinued Operations Stuffing

The accounting standards mandate that the results of those operations scheduled to be discontinued should be shifted below the income from operations line, where it is typically ignored by investors. An easy ploy is for the management team to declare that a business unit is scheduled to be shut down and then tag it as a discontinued operation. Better yet, they stuff all possible expenses into this business unit, thereby increasing the reported profit level from continuing operations. The end result is a total profit figure for the entire business that has not changed, but with a much higher operating profit number.

Cash Flow Reclassifications

The statement of cash flows reveals the cash inflows and outflows of an organization, grouped into sub-categories for cash flows from operations, investing activities, and financing activities. The types of cash flows that are supposed to be associated with these three classifications appear in the following three tables.

Operating Activity Cash Inflows and Outflows

Cash Inflows	Cash Outflows
Cash receipts from the sale of goods and services	Cash payments to employees
Cash receipts from the collection of receivables	Cash payments to suppliers
Cash receipts from lawsuit settlements	Cash payment of fines
Cash receipts from settlement of insurance claims	Cash payments to settle lawsuits
Cash receipts from supplier refunds	Cash payments of taxes
Cash receipts from licensees	Cash refunds to customers
	Cash payments to settle asset retirement obligations
	Cash payment of interest to creditors
	Cash payment of contributions

Investing Activity Cash Inflows and Outflows

Cash Inflows	Cash Outflows
Cash receipts from the sale of equity investments	Cash payments made to acquire equity investments
Cash receipts from the collection of principal on a loan	Cash payments made to acquire debt securities
Cash receipts from the sale of fixed assets	Cash payments made to acquire fixed assets

Financing Activity Cash Inflows and Outflows

Cash Inflows	Cash Outflows
Cash receipts from the sale of company shares	Cash payments to pay dividends
Cash receipts from the issuance of debt instruments	Cash payments to buy back company shares
Cash receipts from a mortgage	Cash payments for debt issuance costs
Cash receipts from derivative instruments	Cash payments to pay down principal on debt

There is a temptation for the management team to bolster the cash flows from operations classification, since this makes the operational activities of the firm appear to be quite robust. To this end, the general goals are:

- To reclassify cash inflows relating to investing and financing activities into the operating activities section; and
- To reclassify cash outflows relating to operating activities into the investing and financing activities section.

Here are several ways in which these goals are accomplished:

- *Buy and sell capacity*. A business can enter into an arrangement where it buys the capacity of its competitors, while also selling competitors its own capacity. The practice was prevalent in the telephone industry at one time. Under this scheme, cash flows received from competitors are classified as cash flows from operating activities, while payments to competitors are classified as cash flows from investing activities.
- *Capitalize operating expenses*. When management incorrectly capitalizes operating expenses, this not only means that the expenditures are now classified as assets on the balance sheet, but also that the cash outflow is now classified as an investing activity, rather than an operating activity.
- *Delay supplier payments*. When payments to suppliers are delayed, this reduces the amount of cash outflows for operating activities. This is not necessarily fraud – a company may simply be abusing its supplier relationships.
- *Make purchases with debt*. A company can acquire goods and services in exchange for a longer-term loan, rather than the usual credit terms that require payment in a month or so. By doing so, the cash outflow (when it occurs) is considered to be the repayment of a loan, which is classified as a financing activity, rather than an operating activity.
- *Retain receivables when selling a subsidiary*. A company could sell a subsidiary while retaining the related receivables, which it then collects. By doing so, the company can recognize the cash inflows related to the receivables as being an operating activity, rather than an investing activity (which would be the classification for the rest of the sale transaction).
- *Sell inventory and buy it back*. When a company enters into an arrangement to sell off its inventory and then buy it back shortly thereafter, this is essentially a loan that uses inventory as collateral. However, because inventory was "sold," the transaction can be mis-characterized as the sale of goods, which then appears as a cash inflow in the operating activity section of the statement of cash flows. The reverse side of the transaction, where the inventory is "bought" back, is then classified as a financing activity.
- *Sell receivables*. A company can validly choose to sell its accounts receivable in order to obtain more immediate use of the related cash. This transaction accelerates the amount of cash inflows reported in the operating activity section. There is nothing illegal about this practice, but it can be misleading, since it accelerates the reported receipt of cash flows into the current period, leaving fewer cash inflows to report in later periods.

Acquisition Falsification

When an organization acquires another business, there are several opportunities to fudge the transaction in the accounting records in order to meet the needs of the acquiring entity. Consider the following:

- *Adjust market values*. An acquirer is supposed to record the assets and liabilities of the acquiree at their market values on the acquisition date. The managers of the acquirer can exert pressure to alter the accounting for this transaction, so that the highest "market value" is assigned to those assets that have the longest depreciable lives, thereby incorrectly extending the period over which expenses will be recognized.
- *Delay sales*. The acquirer in an acquisition arrangement may ask the acquiree to slow down or even halt its recognition of sales in the months leading up to the acquisition date. By doing so, the sales are then recognized after the acquisition date, which allows the acquirer to record a significant boost in its sales.
- *Designation of acquirer*. The designation of the acquirer can be altered, so that the actual acquiree is designated as the acquirer. By doing so, the assets of the "acquiree" can now be marked up to their market values. This approach works from a fraud perspective when there is a clear difference in the potential asset markups between the two entities.

Financial Statement Disclosure Fraud

The accounting standards require that certain additional disclosures be made in addition to the financial statements themselves. These disclosures cover a broad range of topics, and are intended to provide supplemental information that gives the reader a more complete view of the financial performance and condition of a business. Further, a publicly-held company is also required to include in its financial statement reporting the MD&A (management's discussion and analysis) section. The MD&A section describes an organization's opportunities, challenges, risks, trends, future plans, and key performance indicators, as well as changes in revenues, the cost of goods sold, other expenses, assets, and liabilities. These requirements are based on three objectives related to financial reporting, which are:

- To give a narrative explanation of the financial statements from the perspective of management
- To enhance the numerical disclosures in the financial statements, as well as to provide a context within which to review this information
- To discuss the quality and possible variability of an entity's earnings and cash flows

The managers of a business can commit fraud by including incorrect or misleading information in these disclosures, or by not including essential information at all. Here are several examples:

- A company fails to describe the extent to which its sales were boosted by recent acquisitions, leaving investors to assume that the increase was caused by increases in its existing product lines.
- A company does not describe any contingent liabilities, so investors are unaware of the possibility of additional expenditures in the future to settle those liabilities.
- A company does not reveal the existence of long-term purchase obligations, which may create a substantial burden for several years into the future.
- A company targets its sales at lower-income customers, and earns material amounts from them in the form of interest on late payments. The company does not describe the source of this income, leaving investors to assume that the interest income comes from its investments.
- A company sells assets to a related party and buys them back at a later date. The company does not describe the ownership of the other entity, nor does it note the full extent of the arrangement. This is a clear case of disclosure fraud, since the activities that should be disclosed were likely used to pump up the reported sales level.
- A business discloses that there is a contingent gain, when in fact the gain is highly unlikely to occur, and misleads investors into thinking that the company will soon experience a notable windfall.
- A business fails to disclose that it is investing its excess cash in highly risky investments, in hopes of obtaining major returns.

Note: A particular area of concern with disclosure fraud is when a company does not disclose related-party transactions. A related party transaction may comprise a large part of the sales of the company, or the related party may be propping up the business with loans. If these transactions were to be properly reported, the picture presented to the investment community would likely be considerably worse.

Disclosure fraud can occur when the relevant disclosure is indeed present, but the description has been so thoroughly muddled that it is impossible for any but the most discerning reader to understand what is being said.

A variation on the disclosure fraud concept is when a business issues non-GAAP financial information. GAAP (generally accepted accounting principles) mandates that financial information be presented in a certain way that includes all expenses. When a business issues non-GAAP disclosures, it is usually subtracting certain one-time expenses that it does not consider to be relevant, inevitably resulting in a higher profit figure than would have been the case under GAAP reporting.

Another type of disclosure fraud occurs when management thoroughly misrepresents the nature of the business and its products in general informational issuances to the public. These issuances can include press releases, brochures for general distribution, speeches, and its website. This type of fraud is most frequently targeted at prospective investors, to convince them to invest funds in what is effectively a worthless business.

It can be difficult to prove this type of fraud, since it must be intentional. In cases where there is no disclosure at all, and especially when the accounting department is not used to producing detailed disclosures, the error may not be intentional.

Summary

We have presented no preventive controls in this chapter to combat financial statement manipulation, because the management team oversees the control system *and* is usually responsible for altering the financial statements. Instead, fraud prevention needs to originate in other areas. First, there should be an independent board of directors that vigorously oversees operations; this group is not beholden to management, and so can be relied upon to represent other stakeholders. Second, outside auditors, hired by the board of directors, should conduct a comprehensive audit each year. The auditors are in the best position to locate instances of reporting chicanery and report this information back to the board of directors. And finally, the board of directors should remove all incentives for managers to modify the financial statements. This means setting reasonable performance targets for earning bonuses and ensuring that finances are managed conservatively.

Chapter 3
Fraud Schemes by Outsiders

Introduction

Thus far, we have only discussed fraud situations that arise within a business, perpetrated by employees. In addition, organizations are under constant assault from outsiders, who use a variety of techniques to gain access to company assets. These schemes take advantage of any weak spot in a business, such as a need to obtain financing, shortcomings in evaluating the credit of new customers, and inadequate verifications of account change notices. In this chapter, we cover many possible fraud schemes by outsiders, most of which fall under the general headings of imposter schemes, misrepresentation schemes, counterfeit schemes, and money laundering.

Imposter Schemes

One of the most common forms of outsider fraud is for someone to obtain access to company assets by posing as someone else, usually by stealing confidential information about the person. A variation is to obtain credit card information, so that the fraudster can then use the card and impose additional liabilities on the company. Another approach is to gain access to bank account information, with obvious negative effects. Several imposter schemes are noted in the following sub-sections.

Application Fraud

Application fraud occurs when an account is opened using fake or stolen documents, with liabilities being directed at the business. For example, a person could use stolen identification information to open a cell phone account with a local cellular provider, with the charges being billed to the company whose identification information was stolen. At a more aggressive level, someone could pose as a company official in order to obtain a loan from a bank, and then disappears with the funds. The company whose confidential information is being used to perpetrate these types of frauds is probably not liable. However, flip the situation around – what if the company is the cell phone provider or the bank used in the preceding two examples? The company would then be liable for the losses incurred.

It is not easy to detect application fraud, especially when the scammer has multiple forms of identification and falsified documents. However, if the person is rushing to gain approval or wants funds or other assets immediately, the person could be using time pressure in order to keep the company from taking the time normally used to engage in additional verification checks. Consequently, the obvious way to deter application fraud is to build a modest delay into the approval process, so that the approval staff has time to engage in multiple forms of verification.

Bank Account Fraud

Bank account fraud occurs when someone gains access to the user identification and password information for a company's bank account. The person then poses as a valid user to extract funds from the account. For example, a perpetrator can set up a recurring ACH debit transaction to periodically remove funds from a bank account, perhaps to pay for something innocuous, such as a monthly parking fee. Or, the fraud could be on a much larger scale, where the intent is to authorize a large one-time wire transfer out of the account.

Bank account fraud can result in enormous losses, and so requires more extensive controls to minimize the risk of loss. The key controls are preventive in nature, to keep the fraud from ever occurring. For example, require the bank to contact the company whenever a wire transfer greater than a certain threshold is about to be processed. Or, have the bank's systems impose a hard cap of a certain amount on all ACH debits. It is still useful to employ detective controls that spot instances of bank account fraud after the fact, since any items spotted may be recurring, and so can be cut off. For example, an accountant can review the monthly bank statement to see if there are any unusual charges being run through the account.

CEO Fraud

An outsider may be able to make off with a substantial amount of funds when he gains access to the company CEO's e-mail account. The person can then pose as the executive, demanding that funds be wired at once to an outside account in order to complete some sort of false business deal. This scam is especially effective when the outsider knows that the CEO is traveling or on vacation, and so cannot be easily reached by anyone at the office to verify that the demands are valid.

A policy of requiring a phone verification of all wire transfer requests can keep this fraud from occurring.

Redirected Payments Fraud

Redirected payments fraud occurs when an outsider contacts an employee in the accounts payable department, claiming to be an existing supplier and asking the employee to alter an existing recurring bank account debit or other form of payment to a new bank account. This request may also be in the form of an official-looking letter that copies the logo and letterhead of the targeted supplier. If the employee does so, the usual payment amount will still be made, so there will be no indication of a problem until the valid supplier calls to complain that no payments have been made. Since the valid supplier should complain fairly soon, this type of fraud tends to have a relatively short lifespan.

To protect against redirected payments fraud, always verify a request for a payment change, calling an established contact at the supplier. To add an extra level of security, ask the contact at the supplier for the supplier's old bank account information as well, which is information that an outsider is unlikely to have. From a detective perspective, always review the monthly bank statement to see if there are any unusual payments going out to businesses not on the approved supplier list.

Software Service Fraud

Software service fraud is being perpetrated when an outsider contacts employees, stating that credit card information is needed to validate software or install a security update. The people engaging in these scams typically state that they work for a well-known software company, such as Apple or Microsoft, to make them appear more legitimate. If a company procurement card is provided to the caller, the company may now be at risk of illicit purchases being made with the credit card.

Software service scams are best dealt with by training all employees to forward these calls to the information technology department, where a professional can evaluate the situation. If these solicitations arrive by e-mail, instruct employees not to open any attachments, since they might contain malware.

Triangulation Fraud

Triangulation fraud occurs when a fraudster arranges for a legitimate customer to receive a product that the fraudster obtained with a stolen credit card. Under this approach, the fraudster poses as a legitimate seller in order to receive money from the sale of goods. This seller poses as an online reseller of a product that is relatively expensive, and charges an unusually low price for it. This attracts a buyer, who pays for the goods up front. The fraudster then places the buyer's order with a legitimate retailer, using a stolen credit card. The retailer then fills the order, charging its price to the stolen credit card and delivering the goods to the buyer. The buyer cheerfully receives the order, having paid a below-market price for the goods. At this point, the real card holder discovers that his or her card statement contains a fraudulent charge, and files a chargeback claim with their card issuer. The legitimate retailer has to refund the money, but has no recourse to reclaim their product. In short, everyone wins except the legitimate retailer.

This scam is especially hard for the legitimate retailer to spot, since it is charging the normal price to an ostensibly creditworthy customer. Triangulation fraud is a significant concern for the sellers of retail goods; it is less common in other parts of the economy.

Bust-Out Fraud

A common practice for the credit department of a business is to grant small amounts of credit to newer customers, and then gradually build up the amount of credit allowed when there is a history by customers of paying on time. Someone can take advantage of this pattern by setting up a business, placing small orders, and paying the resulting bills within normal terms. At this point, the credit manager is more likely to allow credit for a much larger order. The perpetrator then accepts delivery, shuts down his business, and moves away – without paying the bill. The goods are then liquidated for cash. This is called a bust-out scam.

The process can also work in reverse. The perpetrator sets up a company and begins offering goods at excellent prices, but only when payment is made in advance. Once customers become comfortable with the arrangement, the company offers exceptional pricing for a short period of time in order to attract even larger orders, takes the prepayment money, and walks away from the business.

These arrangements can be quite difficult to spot, since perpetrators are taking advantage of the credit-granting rules of a business to keep from being spotted. A reasonable rule to follow when spotting these situations is the simple maxim that an exceptional price being offered by a business partner probably really is too good to be true.

Misrepresentation Schemes

An outsider can take advantage of a business by offering to provide goods or services and then either not providing them or providing a sub-standard product. These schemes work especially well when a company is desperate for the goods or services in question, has little experience in obtaining a particular specialized service, or has weak purchasing controls. Several misrepresentation schemes are noted in the following sub-sections.

Advance-Fee Loan Fraud

A business may have difficulty obtaining a loan through normal sources, perhaps due to a poor record of previous loan repayments, or poor fundamentals in its financial statements that are scaring away traditional lenders. If so, the owners may examine alternatives that are essentially fraud schemes. These schemes usually involve the offer of a guaranteed loan if the company first pays a fee. The perpetrator promises to represent the business with a recognized lender, saying that he has the connections needed to secure a loan. Once the fee is paid, the person either vanishes or puts off the firm with various excuses.

A variation on the concept is to require a fee to obtain an introduction to a lender. In this case, the fee agreement may be structured so that there is no actual fraud – the business is simply paying for a referral. If the lender to which the business is being referred then demands an exorbitant fee, the referring person can claim to only being responsible for the initial introduction.

In an advance-fee scheme, the fee is frequently stated as a percentage of the gross amount of the loan that the organization is trying to obtain. For example, a 5% fee might be charged in order to secure a $100,000 loan, so the person is paid a $5,000 fee. When the business is only paying for an introduction, the payment is more likely to be a fixed sum, such as $10,000.

A reasonable degree of caution will keep a business from falling into this type of scheme. A key preventive point is to consider why a promoter can obtain a loan on the company's behalf when it is impossible to do so directly. Also, be sure to obtain the name of the lender that will be extending a loan, and verify with that lender the representations made by the promoter. In addition, ask for contact information for other entities that have used the promoter in the past, and contact them to see if they actually obtained the promised loan amounts. Finally, conduct a background investigation on the promoter to see if there have been any issues with him in the past, or if there are indicators of fraud in his prior business dealings.

Investor Marketing Fraud

An investment advisory firm purports to be able to market a fledging public company's stock to investors, in exchange for either a cash payment or a certain number of company shares. The extent of the firm's marketing efforts is likely to be an e-mail list, to which it attaches a brief summary of the company and its prospects. Since the e-mail burst is usually tagged by e-mail servers as spam, it is rarely read by investors. Thus, *some* activity is occurring on behalf of the company, but at a level that is likely to be well below the company's expectations. This fraud persists because small public companies have so little experience in building relations with investors.

It is difficult to prevent this fraud, since investor marketing deals are usually entered into by the CEO or CFO, who may be desperate to build trading volume in company shares, and so will grasp at even the most flimsy marketing offers. If they can be encouraged to let these proposed deals sit for a few weeks, they will have time to consider whether the company will be receiving sufficient value in exchange for the price paid.

Business Directory Fraud

An organization may receive a notice from a supposed publisher of an industry directory, asking whether the company wants to be listed. If the company responds in any way, the "publisher" sends an invoice – usually for an overblown amount – to pay for the listing. A further fraud may be that there is no directory at all, or the directory is only published in small quantities and is not delivered to any valuable users. This type of fraud is particularly insidious when the company initially pays the billed amount, so the "publisher" continues to send recurring invoices. Since the payables staff sees the earlier payments in the accounting system, they assume that these payments are legitimate and continue paying the invoices.

There are several ways to combat business directory fraud. One approach is to conduct an annual review of all marketing expenses, going over the bills with the marketing director, to see if any items being paid are not for real services. A more proactive approach is to mandate that all proposed marketing services be forwarded to the marketing director for approval – who is presumably capable of spotting nefarious business directory offers.

Substandard Goods Fraud

A supplier may sell low-grade goods to a business, charging a price normally associated with substantially higher-quality products. The fraud lies in the misrepresentation of the goods as being of a normal level of quality. For example, a supplier calls a company's receptionist and asks if it can supply the firm's toner cartridges for its copier. If the receptionist gives an answer that can even remotely be construed as being "yes," the supplier immediately drops off low-grade toner cartridges at the company's receiving dock and demands immediate payment.

Substandard goods can be ferreted out by any reasonably efficient purchasing department, so suppliers work around the purchasing department by targeting non-purchasing personnel, frequently in the administrative area. The solutions are both preventive and detective. From the perspective of prevention, all employees are instructed to forward all supplier communications to the purchasing department. From a detective perspective, any instance of substandard goods fraud calls for immediate follow-up with the person who allegedly approved the purchase, to ensure that they do not do so again.

Counterfeit Schemes

Outsiders may copy the goods, services, and marketing promotions of a company, selling them at a discount to unsuspecting customers. The company is not always directly impacted by these schemes, but may lose sales as a result of the counterfeiting activities. Several of these situations are noted next.

Counterfeit Goods Fraud

An organization may be secondarily subject to a counterfeit goods fraud. A scammer creates goods that look like an entity's products, but which are of inferior quality, and sells them to customers. The customers are the primary targets. If the goods subsequently fail, the customers may present them to the organization for replacement or repair, at which point the customer service staff must spend time reviewing the presented goods and dealing with frustrated customers. Counterfeit goods fraud has an additional secondary impact on a company, which is that the fake goods are cannibalizing sales that the company might otherwise have made.

Counterfeit goods fraud is especially pernicious for high-end consumer goods, where counterfeit goods can be easily manufactured in less-regulated countries and then distributed over the globe for sale. This fraud is not easy to combat, requiring cooperative efforts with the police forces having jurisdiction in the areas where the goods are being produced and sold.

Gift Certificate Fraud

An organization may be subject to gift certificate fraud if it sells gift certificates. A fraudster creates fake gift certificates and sells them to customers, who then present them to the company for use in purchasing goods or services. If the receiving employee does not recognize that these certificates are fraudulent, then they are used to pay all or part of the amount payable by the customer, resulting in a loss by the company.

There are several ways to mitigate the risk of this type of fraud. First, train employees to recognize valid gift certificates, showing them the security features to look for. Second, imprint a unique identification code on each certificate, which is verified at the point of presentation by a customer. In both cases, rejecting a fake gift certificate means that the loss is shifted to the customer, who originally bought the gift certificate.

Inbound Check Fraud

A company has been subjected to check fraud when it is paid with a stolen check or one for which there are insufficient funds. In this case, the firm will receive a notification from its bank that there are not sufficient funds (NSF) to deposit a presented check. Alternatively, if the company is paid with a stolen check, it may receive a notification from the rightful owner of the check stock that was stolen.

It can be quite difficult to minimize the losses from inbound check fraud. A proper credit screening of new customers will keep away those people that have a history of passing bad checks, while only granting minimal initial credit levels to new customers can minimize the amount of losses that may be incurred.

Money Laundering Schemes

Money laundering is the process of obscuring the origins of illegally-obtained cash, so that it appears to be legitimate. By using money laundering, one can avoid the risk of having cash appropriated by the government.

The basic concept behind money laundering schemes is to shift illegally-obtained cash into a different entity, usually in another country, and then convert it into legal assets. The process works best when the cash is shifted through a series of other entities in multiple countries, thereby making it more difficult to ascertain the origins of the cash.

Once the cash has been shifted through the bank accounts of a sufficient number of enterprises, it is invested in an entity that is entirely legitimate, such as a restaurant, office building, farm, or manufacturing facility.

The best money laundering schemes involve shifting funds through numerous people, thereby making it more difficult for anyone to associate funds obtained by one party as being the funds now held by someone else. The risk to the money launderer is that one of these parties will abscond with the cash, so hefty fees or commissions are allowed as money shifts through the various entities that are laundering money.

The basic steps in a money laundering scheme are as follows:

1. *Placement in a financial institution.* Cash is deposited in bank accounts. This can be difficult, since banks are required to notify the government of large cash deposits. Accordingly, deposits are made in small and irregularly-sized amounts, using a variety of accounts at different banks. Also, bank officials may be bribed to not report these cash deposits.
2. *Cash movement.* Once deposited, the cash is transferred in differing amounts to many other accounts in banks in several other countries, with the intent of making the transfers as difficult to follow as possible. Examples of the ways in which this cash movement is conducted are:

   - *Underground banking.* There are undocumented "underground banking" systems in some countries that do not report their transactions to

42

the government. Money is shifted into and out of these banking systems.

- *Shell companies.* Shell companies are created that offer fake goods and services in exchange for cash. Once received, this cash is the property of the shell company, which is likely to be under the control of the original cash owner or an associate.
- *Legitimate businesses.* Cash is injected into a legitimate business by having that business bill for additional revenues and paying it with laundered cash.
- *Asset purchases.* The form of the cash is changed into some type of asset, such as real estate, jewelry, paintings, and so forth.
- *Currency conversion.* Cash is exchanged into a different currency, possibly going through several conversions, in order to hide its origins.

3. *Cash conversion.* Once the origins of the cash have been sufficiently obscured, it is used to purchase assets, varying from commodities to real estate. This represents the "cleaned" version of the cash - it cannot be traced, and it appears to be legitimate. At this point, the cash can be used by the actual owner.

Money laundering operations can be quite complex, requiring the services of lawyers, bankers, and accountants to continually dream up new laundering schemes and keep track of the flow of money.

Money laundering can result in unusual transactions that serve as red flags. For example:

- Owning expensive assets without an obvious source of wealth to pay for them
- Paying for expensive assets in cash
- Paying for ongoing expenses in cash
- Using a corporation to buy assets that are obviously for personal use
- Using an unusual number of cashier's checks or money orders

Fraud Tools used by Outsiders

An outsider needs access to a company's confidential information in order to engage in the imposter schemes noted earlier in this chapter. This information can be collected via social engineering fraud. Also, the bust-out fraud noted earlier is best accomplished with a temporary business address. Both of these fraud tools are noted in the following sub-sections.

Social Engineering Fraud

A business is being subjected to social engineering fraud when an outsider tricks an employee into divulging confidential information about the organization. This information is then used to extract assets from the business. Different types of this fraud are noted in the following bullet points:

- *Phishing*. Phishing involves a communication of any type from an outsider, with the intent of tricking the recipient into divulging login credentials or account information. These communications may be structured to look exceedingly authentic, using logos and other information extracted from the website of the entity being faked.
- *Spoofing*. Spoofing involves a communication (usually an e-mail) being sent from an unknown third party, disguised as a source known to the recipient. This message may request that the person respond with an account number for verification purposes, which the recipient then accesses. The message could also request that the person click on a link, which downloads malware onto the person's computer.
- *Smishing*. Smishing is the same as spoofing, except that the recipient receives the message via a text message. The result is usually the downloading of malware onto the recipient's phone.
- *Vishing*. Vishing involves the use of phone calls, supposedly from a reputable party, to extract information from the recipient, such as bank account and credit card information.

We have just noted that malware may be downloaded onto a person's computer or phone. The intent of this malware from a fraud perspective is to log the keystrokes of the victim, so that user identifications and passwords can be extracted and sent to the outsider.

There are several ways to detect and prevent social engineering fraud. Foremost on the list is to verify any requests made in person or by calling a trusted individual. Another alternative is to examine any messages sent for typos, poor graphics quality and the like, indicating that the message is false. And in general, employees should be trained to be suspicious of any unusual requests for payment, and should never click on any e-mail or text message links or attachments.

Temporary Business Address

Someone trying to commit fraud can temporarily rent space or just a mailbox in a prestigious location. For example, he could rent an office by the month, with a receptionist who takes calls for a group of these temporary offices. By doing so, he is creating a false impression that his business is long-established and well-funded. An organization dealing with this individual could be mis-led into believing that the entity is a valid one, making it easier for the individual to perpetrate fraud.

The use of a temporary business address is a baseline function that can be used to engage in several possible types of fraud – it is not, by itself, a fraudulent activity. An indicator that a temporary address is being used to engage in fraud is when a legitimate organization is asked to send funds to the temporary address, perhaps as an advance on a purchase arrangement. The person operating the temporary address then pockets the money and terminates the office or mailbox rental arrangement. Another fraudulent use of this arrangement is when a person offers the founders of a new business to operate out of his offices, at which point the incoming mail of the new business is intercepted and payments extracted.

There are several ways to deal with people using temporary business addresses. One approach is to run a credit report on all prospective business partners, to see how long they have been in business at their current location. One can also conduct an Internet search on the address, to see if it is advertised as being a rent-an-office location. A third option is to have a policy of only making advance payments with the approval of senior management, or only after having done business with another party for at least a year.

Summary

Any business is under constant assault by outsiders, constantly probing for confidential information and other ways in which to scam the company into parting with its assets. The usual focus of a system of controls will ensure that normal company processes will be handled in a consistent manner, but those controls are not as well designed to deal with potential fraud situations – especially when the weak point in the system of control is employees. For example, it is far too easy for employees to be conned into entering bank account access codes into a well-constructed e-mail, and for a desperate CFO to agree to an up-front loan fee that never results in a loan. A good way to reduce the number of these events is to use the information in this chapter as the basis for a presentation to new employees, informing them of the fraud schemes to which they may be subjected on an ongoing basis by outsiders.

Glossary

A

Amortization. The ratable charging of assets to expense over a period of time.

B

Balance sheet. A financial statement that presents information about an entity's assets, liabilities, and shareholders' equity.

Bid rigging. Inside assistance given to a supplier to win a bidding process, usually in exchange for a kickback.

Bust-out scam. The practice of building up credit with a company, then placing a large order for a substantial amount of goods, and walking away without paying.

C

Contingent liability. A possible obligation that depends on future events that are not under an entity's control.

F

Financial statements. A collection of reports about an organization's financial results, financial position, and cash flows.

Fraud. A false representation of the facts, resulting in the object of the fraud receiving an injury by acting upon the misrepresented facts.

G

Gross profit. This is the residual amount after the cost of goods sold is subtracted from sales.

I

Income statement. A financial statement that contains the results of an organization's operations for a specific period of time, showing revenues and expenses and the resulting profit or loss.

K

Kickback. When a supplier pays a buyer a bribe in exchange for selecting the supplier to supply goods and services to the buyer's company.

L

Lapping. When an employee steals cash by diverting a payment from one customer, and then hides the theft by diverting cash from another customer to offset the receivable from the first customer.

M

Money laundering. The process of altering the sources of cash so that it appears to come from a legitimate source.

P

Profit. The amount by which sales exceed expenses.

R

Revenue recognition. The process of determining the amount and timing of when revenue is recognized, based on the underlying earnings process.

S

Segregation of duties. The division of a task into multiple parts, so that more than one person is required to complete the task.

Skimming. The removal of cash from a system before it can be recorded.

Social engineering. The psychological manipulation of people, so that they will divulge information or perform other actions not in their best interests.

Statement of cash flows. A financial statement that identifies the different types of cash payments made by a business to third parties (cash outflows), as well as payments made to a business by third parties (cash inflows).

Stock option. A financial instrument that gives its holder the right, but not the obligation, to buy shares at a certain price and within a certain date range.

T

Topside entry. A manual adjusting entry made at the corporate level.

Index